First Facts®

The Solar System

Space Tourism

by Steve Kortenkamp

Consultant:
James Gerard
Aerospace Education Specialist, NASA
Kennedy Space Center, Florida

Capstone
press®

Mankato, Minnesota

First Facts is published by Capstone Press,
151 Good Counsel Drive, P.O. Box 669, Mankato, Minnesota 56002.
www.capstonepress.com

Library of Congress Cataloging-in-Publication Data
Kortenkamp, Steve.
    Space tourism / by Steve Kortenkamp.
    p. cm. — (First facts. The solar system)
    Summary: "Describes the training and activities of past space tourists and explores how
companies may take tourists to space in the future" — Provided by publisher.
    Includes bibliographical references and index.
    ISBN–13: 978–1–4296–1260–9 (hardcover)
    ISBN–10: 1–4296–1260–6 (hardcover)
    1. Space tourism — Juvenile literature. I. Title. II. Series.
TL793.K663 2008
910.919 — dc22   2007023031

Editorial Credits

Lori Shores and Christopher L. Harbo, editors; Juliette Peters, set designer; Kim Brown, book
    designer and illustrator; Linda Clavel, photo researcher

Photo Credits

Bigelow Aerospace, 18
DreamSpace and The da Vinci Project, 13 (top left)
NASA, 1, 20, 21
Photodisc, back cover
Rocketplane Global, 13 (bottom left)
Scaled Composites, LLC, 14; Aero-News Network/Jim Campbell,15
Shimizu Corporation, cover
Space Adventures, 5, 8, 9, 10, 11
Starchaser Industries Ltd, 13 (right)
Virgin Galactic, 17

1 2 3 4 5 6 13 12 11 10 09 08

Table of Contents

The First Space Tourist

Some **tourists** climb mountains to stand on top of the world. Others travel to Antarctica to be on the bottom. Space tourists take trips that are out of this world! In 2001, Dennis Tito became the first space tourist when he visited the *International Space Station*.

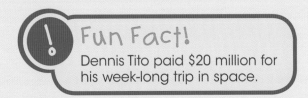

Fun Fact!
Dennis Tito paid $20 million for his week-long trip in space.

Dennis Tito

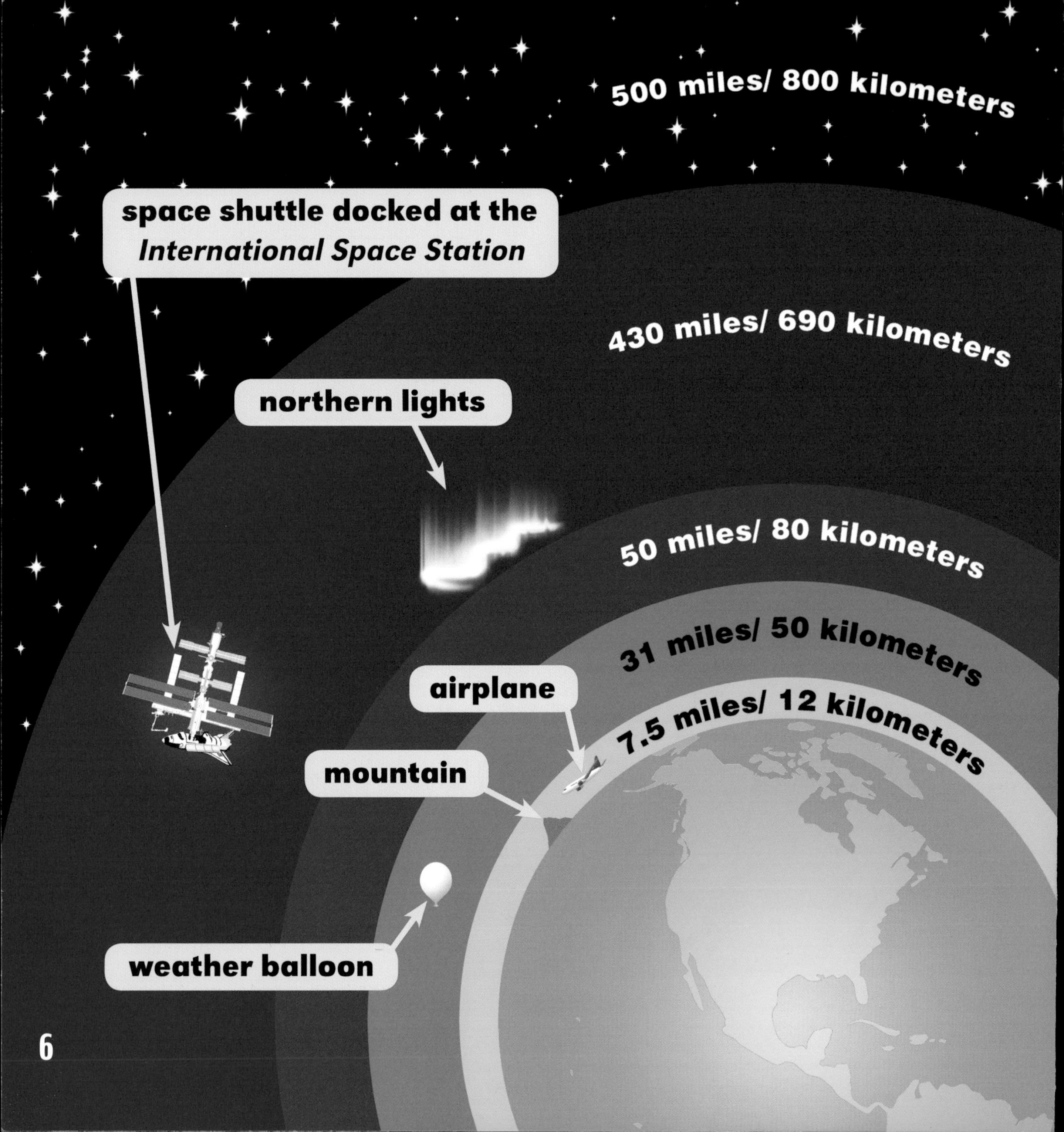

500 miles/ 800 kilometers

space shuttle docked at the *International Space Station*

430 miles/ 690 kilometers

northern lights

50 miles/ 80 kilometers

31 miles/ 50 kilometers

airplane

7.5 miles/ 12 kilometers

mountain

weather balloon

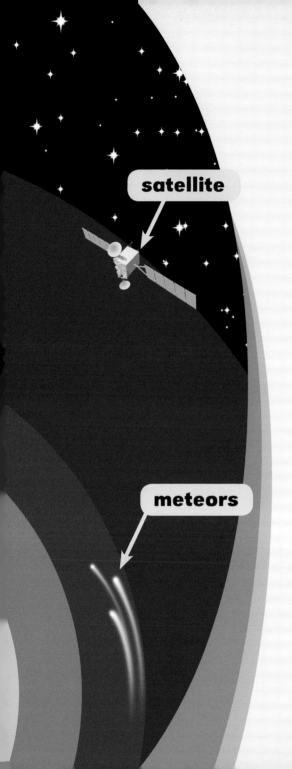

satellite

meteors

How High Is Space?

Outer space begins about 50 miles (80 kilometers) above Earth. Airplanes can't fly that high. Space tourists must ride rockets to the space station. The space station **orbits** Earth at a distance of 200 miles (322 kilometers) away.

Fun Fact!
Most airplanes fly about 6 miles (10 kilometers) from Earth.

Training for a Space Vacation

Before going into space, tourists train for about a year. They use machines that spin very fast. The machines let them feel what a rocket launch is like.

Space tourists also train on airplanes that make steep dives. During the dives people inside the plane feel **weightless**. They'll feel the same way in space.

Working Vacations

Space tourists do more than just look out the window and take pictures. Greg Olsen and Mark Shuttleworth worked on science **experiments**.

Greg Olsen

Anousheh Ansari

In 2006, Anousheh Ansari became the first female space tourist. She did experiments too. She studied **germs** and mold that grow at the space station.

The Race to Space

The first space tourists used Russian rockets to reach space. In the future, private companies will take people into space. To make this happen, Anousheh Ansari's family helped create the Ansari X-Prize contest. Companies competed to make a reusable rocket for space tourism. The winning company received a prize of $10 million.

Fun Fact!

To win the X-Prize, a rocket had to be able to launch three people into space twice in two weeks.

Wild Fire MK V1

V-Tail Earthv2

Starchaser

13

White Knight

SpaceShipOne

In 2004, a spacecraft named *SpaceShipOne* won the Ansari X-Prize. An airplane named *White Knight* carried *SpaceShipOne* high up into the air. Then *SpaceShipOne* was let go.

The pilot of *SpaceShipOne* fired a rocket that sent the spacecraft straight up. After the rocket ran out of fuel, *SpaceShipOne* coasted into space.

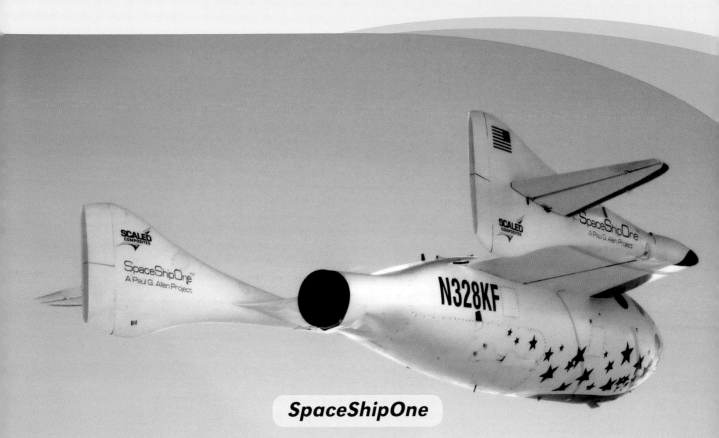

SpaceShipOne

Instead of going into orbit, rockets like *SpaceShipOne* make **suborbital flights** into space. They go straight up and straight back down.

SpaceShipOne carried only a pilot. A new spacecraft named *SpaceShipTwo* is being built. It will carry six tourists into space at the same time.

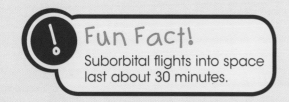

Fun Fact!
Suborbital flights into space last about 30 minutes.

SpaceShipTwo

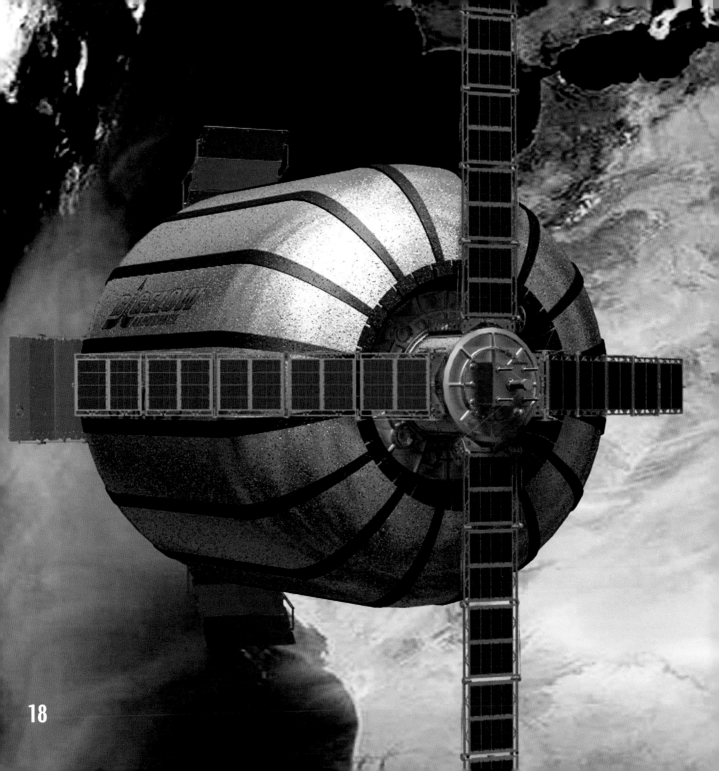

Hotels in Space

In the future, space tourists may stay overnight in space. One company is working to build a space **hotel**. When the hotel reaches orbit, its rooms will inflate like balloons. Tourists may use space hotels to enjoy the view of Earth. Others may rest at space hotels before traveling to the Moon or beyond.

Amazing but True!

Someday, tourists might be able to ride elevators up into space. A space elevator could have a long cable that starts on the ground. The cable would stretch up to a space station. Elevator cars would climb up the cable to carry people and machines into space.

Think Big!

The first space tourists went to the *International Space Station*. Soon other tourists will take suborbital flights on *SpaceShipTwo*. Someday space tourists might stay in orbiting hotels, or even travel to the Moon. If you were a space tourist, where would you go?

Glossary

experiment (ek-SPER-uh-ment) — a scientific test to find out how something works

germ (JURM) — a very small living thing that can cause disease

hotel (hoh-TEL) — a place where travelers pay to stay overnight

orbit (OR-bit) — to travel around a planet or any other object in space

suborbital flight (SUB-or-bit-ahl FLITE) — a flight into space that is too slow to orbit Earth

tourist (TOOR-ist) — a person who travels and visits places for fun or adventure

weightless (WATE-liss) — free of the feeling of gravity

Read More

Kerrod, Robin. *Space Stations.* The History of Space Exploration. Milwaukee: World Almanac Library, 2005.

Solway, Andrew. *Can We Travel to the Stars?: Space Flight and Space Exploration.* Stargazers' Guides. Chicago: Heinemann, 2006.

Whitehouse, Patricia. *Living in Space.* Space Explorer. Chicago: Heinemann, 2004.

Internet Sites

FactHound offers a safe, fun way to find Internet sites related to this book. All of the sites on FactHound have been researched by our staff.

Here's how:
1. Visit *www.facthound.com*
2. Choose your grade level.
3. Type in this book ID **1429612606** for age-appropriate sites. You may also browse subjects by clicking on letters, or by clicking on pictures and words.
4. Click on the **Fetch It** button.

Facthound will fetch the best sites for you!

23

Index